TABLE OF CO

T0015151

CHAPTER 1

SLOW SWIMMERS

What small sea creature is one of the world's slowest swimmers? It is a seahorse! Its head looks like a horse's head.

THE WORLD OF OCEAN ANIMALS
SEAHORSES

by Mari Schuh

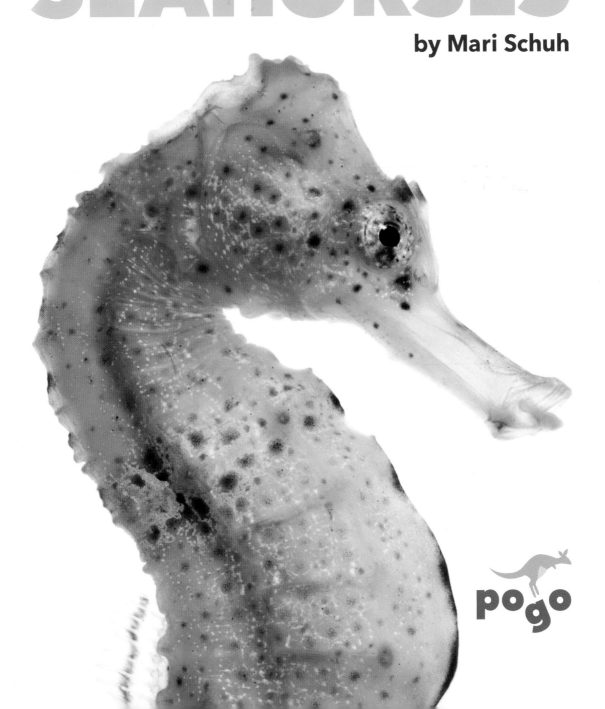

pogo

Ideas for Parents and Teachers

Pogo Books let children practice reading informational text while introducing them to nonfiction features such as headings, labels, sidebars, maps, and diagrams, as well as a table of contents, glossary, and index.

Carefully leveled text with a strong photo match offers early fluent readers the support they need to succeed.

Before Reading

- "Walk" through the book and point out the various nonfiction features. Ask the student what purpose each feature serves.
- Look at the glossary together. Read and discuss the words.

Read the Book

- Have the child read the book independently.
- Invite him or her to list questions that arise from reading.

After Reading

- Discuss the child's questions. Talk about how he or she might find answers to those questions.
- Prompt the child to think more. Ask: Seahorses are fish. But they are different from most fish. What are some ways seahorses are different from other fish?

Pogo Books are published by Jump!
5357 Penn Avenue South
Minneapolis, MN 55419
www.jumplibrary.com

Copyright © 2024 Jump!
International copyright reserved in all countries. No part of this book may be reproduced in any form without written permission from the publisher.

Library of Congress Cataloging-in-Publication Data

Names: Schuh, Mari C., 1975- author.
Title: Seahorses / by Mari Schuh.
Description: Minneapolis, MN: Jump!, Inc., [2024]
Series: The world of ocean animals | Includes index.
Audience: Ages 7-10
Identifiers: LCCN 2023001911 (print)
LCCN 2023001912 (ebook)
ISBN 9798885245746 (hardcover)
ISBN 9798885245753 (paperback)
ISBN 9798885245760 (ebook)
Subjects: LCSH: Sea horses–Juvenile literature.
Classification: LCC QL638.S9 S365 2024 (print)
LCC QL638.S9 (ebook)
DDC 597/.6798–dc23/eng/20230126
LC record available at https://lccn.loc.gov/2023001911
LC ebook record available at https://lccn.loc.gov/2023001912

Editor: Jenna Gleisner
Designer: Molly Ballanger

Photo Credits: ELENA SANCHEZ/iStock, cover; Eric Isselee/Shutterstock, 1; tbradford/iStock, 3; Kjeld Friis/Shutterstock, 4; Vladimir Turkenich/Shutterstock, 5; Katherine Obrien/iStock, 6-7; kaschibo/Shutterstock, 7; Marevision/age fotostock/SuperStock, 8-9; Zepherwind/Dreamstime, 10-11; sergemi/Shutterstock, 12; Sait Ozgur Gedikoglu/Shutterstock, 13; Krzysztof Bargiel/Dreamstime, 14-15; Zhane Luk/Shutterstock, 16 (left); skynesher/iStock, 16 (right); Photoshot/SuperStock, 17; Tony Wu/Nature Picture Library/SuperStock, 18-19; Doug Perrine/Nature Picture Library, 20-21; Rich Carey/Shutterstock, 23.

Printed in the United States of America at Corporate Graphics in North Mankato, Minnesota.

spine

There are at least 47 seahorse **species**. They can be different colors. Most have stripes or spots. Some have **spines**.

big-belly
seahorse

They come in many sizes.
A pygmy seahorse is as small
as a lima bean. A big-belly
seahorse is more than one
foot (0.3 meters) long!

pygmy
seahorse

Seahorses are fish. But unlike most fish, seahorses do not have **scales**. They are covered with hard plates. The plates make it tough for **predators** like crabs to eat them.

TAKE A LOOK!

What are the parts of a seahorse? Take a look!

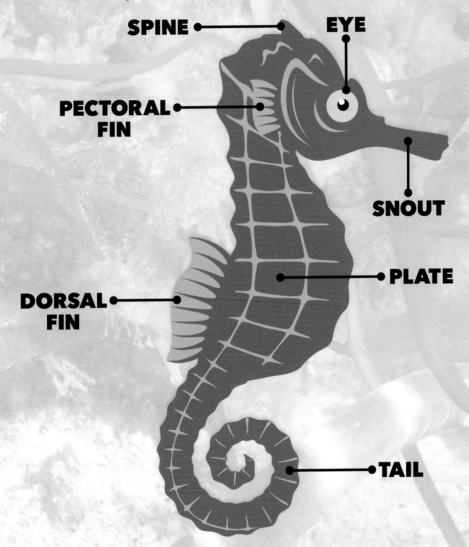

SPINE

EYE

PECTORAL FIN

SNOUT

DORSAL FIN

PLATE

TAIL

Seahorses swim upright. This makes it hard for them to move quickly through the water. Their tails do not have fins. Their dorsal fins help them move forward. Pectoral fins help them **steer**.

DID YOU KNOW?

Seahorses can move up and down. How? They change the amount of air in their swim bladder. This is an air sac inside their body. More air in the sac makes the seahorse float. Less air makes the seahorse sink.

dorsal fin

pectoral fin

CHAPTER 2

HIDING IN THE OCEAN

A seahorse's tail wraps around seagrass. The seahorse changes colors. It uses this **camouflage** to blend in. Now it is hard for predators and **prey** to see it.

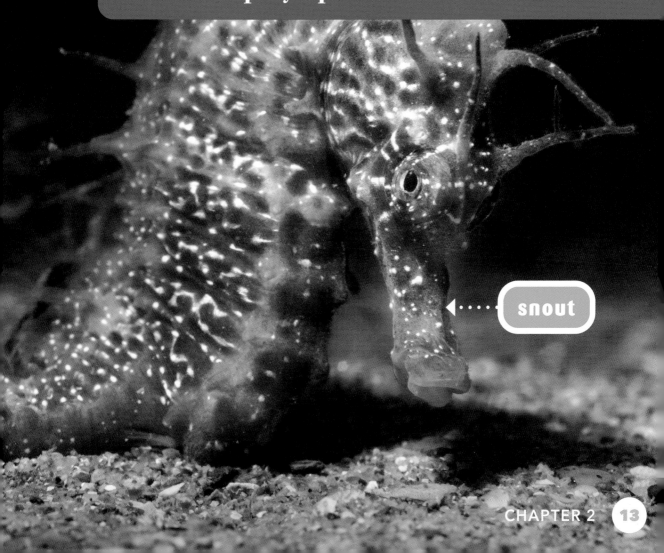

Seahorses hide and wait for prey like **plankton** and small shrimp. When prey swims by, a seahorse pushes its head forward. Its long, narrow snout quietly moves closer. The prey does not notice. Then, like a vacuum, the seahorse sucks the prey up!

snout

Seahorses live in **shallow** ocean water near the **coast**. The water is calm and warm. Most of the time, seahorses stay still. Their tails hold onto plants and **corals**. This keeps them from floating away.

Where do seahorses live? Take a look!

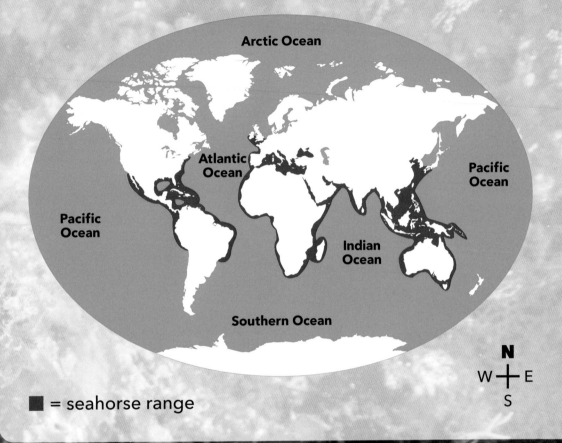

■ = seahorse range

CHAPTER 3

YOUNG SEAHORSES

Seahorses sometimes use their tails to hold onto one another. Before seahorses **mate**, they dance together. A male and female turn and spin.

brood
pouch

The female can lay hundreds of eggs! She puts them in the male's **brood pouch**.

The male's belly grows. He carries the eggs for up to 45 days. Then, it is time to give birth. The male bends and squeezes. This pushes young seahorses out of his pouch. The young are called fry. Fry often look like tiny adults. They are the size of jelly beans!

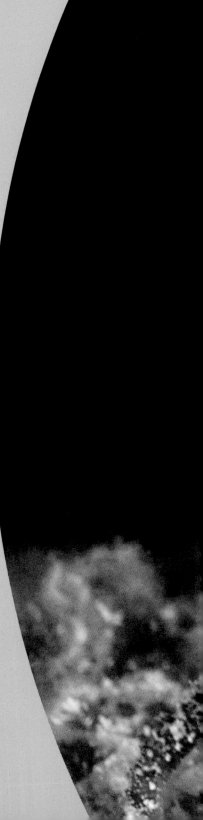

fry

The fry never go back in the pouch. They live on their own and look for their own food. When they grow up, each seahorse finds its own **territory** to live in.

> ## DID YOU KNOW?
>
> Seahorses can travel long distances. Some travel more than 3,000 miles (4,800 kilometers). How? They go for a ride! Their tail grabs onto floating seaweed or other floating plants.

ACTIVITIES & TOOLS

TRY THIS!

FLOATING AND SINKING

A seahorse adds air to its swim bladder to float in the water. Try this fun activity to learn more!

What You Need:

- one orange
- large bowl or tub
- water
- notebook
- pen or pencil

1. Fill a large bowl or tub almost full of water.

2. Do you think the orange will float or sink in the water when you place it in? Write your prediction in your notebook.

3. Gently place the orange in the water. What happens? Does it float or sink?

4. Take the orange out of the water.

5. Peel the orange. If you need help, ask an adult.

6. Do you think the peeled orange will float or sink? Write your prediction in your notebook.

7. Place the peeled orange in the water. What happens? Does it float or sink? An orange peel has air pockets in it. These air pockets help the orange float. How is this like a seahorse's swim bladder?

GLOSSARY

brood pouch: A pocket or sac on a male seahorse that holds eggs.

camouflage: A disguise or natural coloring that allows animals to hide by making them look like their surroundings.

coast: The land next to an ocean or sea.

corals: Substances found underwater that are made up of tiny sea creature skeletons.

mate: To join together to produce young.

plankton: Tiny animals and plants that float in oceans and lakes.

predators: Animals that hunt other animals for food.

prey: Animals that are hunted by other animals for food.

scales: Thin, flat, overlapping pieces of hard skin that cover the bodies of fish or reptiles.

shallow: Not deep.

species: One of the groups into which similar animals and plants are divided.

spines: Hard, sharp, pointed growths on a seahorse that help protect it from predators.

steer: To make something move in a particular direction.

territory: The area an animal lives in and protects.

INDEX

TO LEARN MORE

Finding more information is as easy as 1, 2, 3.

① Go to www.factsurfer.com

② Enter "seahorses" into the search box.

③ Choose your book to see a list of websites.

FACT SURFER